P9-CQA-788

STEVE JOBS

STEVE JOBS

insanely great

a graphic biography by jessie hartland

schwartz & wade books · new york

All rights reserved. Published in the United States by Schwartz & Wade Books,
an imprint of Penguin Random House LLC, New York.
Schwartz & Wade Books and the colophon are trademarks of Penguin Random House LLC.

Library of Congress Cataloging-in-Publication Data
Hartland, Jessie.
Steve Jobs : insanely great / Jessie Hartland. — First edition.
pages cm
Includes bibliographical references and index.
ISBN 978-0-307-98295-7 (alk. paper) — ISBN 978-0-307-98297-1 (ebook)
1. Jobs, Steve, 1955–2011. 2. Jobs, Steve, 1955–2011—Comic books, strips, etc.
3. Computer engineers—United States—Biography. 4. Computer engineers—
United States—Biography—Comic books, strips, etc. 5. Graphic novels. I. Title.
QA76.2.J63 H37 2015
338.761004092—dc23
[B]
2014005768

The text of this book was lettered by hand.
The illustrations were rendered in brush, India ink, and black pencil.
Book design by Rachael Cole and Brianne Farley

Printed in the United States of America
10 9 8 7 6 5 4 3 2 1
First Edition

This one's for
my son, Sam —
lover of apple pie
as well as those
other, nonedible
~~apple~~ products.

Contents

Here's to the crazy ones. The misfits. The rebels. The troublemakers. The square pegs in the round holes. The ones who see things differently. Because the people who are crazy enough to think they can change the world are the ones who do.

— S.J.

the journey
is the reward
— S. J.

STEVE JOBS

He was a tinkerer. He was willful and rebellious and did NOT like to follow rules.

He was a techno-geek and an artist.

He dropped out of college after just one semester and took a calligraphy class.

He brought us the COOL products everyone wants, and award-winning films like Toy Story, UP, and Finding Nemo.

He started Apple Computer in his parents' garage and it became the world's most valuable company.

How did such an iconoclast become the world's best businessman? This is the story.

iPad

Steve's Bench

chapter

1

The

Young Sprout

(1955 - 1965)

Steve is born in San Francisco, California, in 1955.

His biological parents are unmarried college students.

They put Steve up for adoption.

Later, they marry and have a daughter, whom they raise; then they divorce.

Steve is adopted by Clara and Paul Jobs.

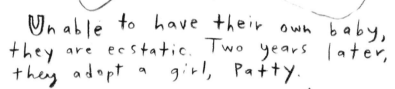

Unable to have their own baby, they are ecstatic. Two years later, they adopt a girl, Patty.

Steve grows up in the Santa Clara Valley (now Silicon* Valley), south of San Francisco.

"a Likeler"

They live in a tract home inspired by the developer Joseph Eichler: simple, modern, suburban.

---

*a common element found in sand and glass, used in making high-tech devices

From an early age, Steve is mischievous. He is a rule-breaker, big-time. In elementary school he creates some posters.

Bring your PET to school day Tomorrow!

Ha Ha

P Q R S T U V W X Y Z

The next day is CRAZY!!

Paul Jobs is a machinist. He makes *prototypes* in the technology industry and his hobby is fixing up cars.

JUNK YARD

FORD

Steve and his dad like to tinker. Many weekends they visit the junkyard and pick up odds and ends for projects they make in their garage.

FORD

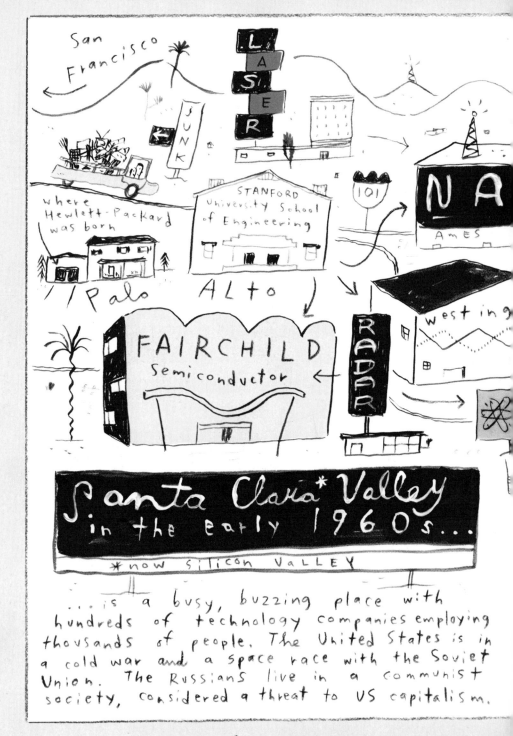

San Francisco

LASER

JUNK

where Hewlett-Packard was born

STANFORD University School of Engineering

101

NA

AmES

Palo ALto

FAIRCHILD Semiconductor

RADAR

west ing

Santa Clara* Valley in the early 1960s...

*now Silicon VaLLEY

...is a busy, buzzing place with hundreds of technology companies employing thousands of people. The United States is in a cold war and a space race with the Soviet Union. The Russians live in a communist society, considered a threat to US capitalism.

6

Santa Clara Mountains

San Jose →

MISSILES

Lockheed Missiles and Space Division

S A
Research Center

AMPEX

El Camino Real

Hewlett-Packard
Technical Instruments

HP

ouse

Batteries

Spectra-Physics

Los Altos

FORD

Having launched Sputnik, the first satellite, in 1957, the Soviets are winning the space race. Scrambling to catch up, the US government is funding oodles of defense contractors who are experimenting with new space and weapons technology. These Silicon Valley businesses are part of what's called the military-industrial complex.

Steve's neighborhood is swarming with engineers who work at places like NASA, Westinghouse, and Lockheed Missile.

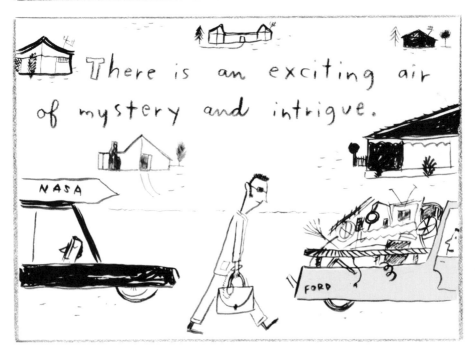

There is an exciting air of mystery and intrigue.

NASA

FORD

Companies that started out small inside home garages, like nearby Hewlett-Packard, are becoming giant. Tiny new companies are sprouting up in Steve's neighborhood.

One day they will be huge.

Steve and his dad make good use of their garage.

Steve even has his own workbench.

One weekend they build a wooden fence around their yard.

Even the parts you can't see should be well made and look good.

OK, Dad.

Fine craftsmanship is important to Steve's dad.

Steve likes to assemble do-it-yourself kits. It makes him feel like he can build ANYTHING.

Steve learns at an early age that he is adopted.

His parents reassure him:

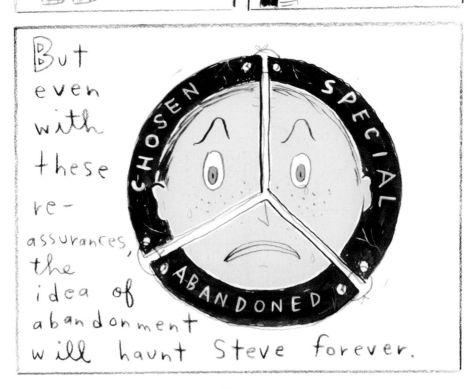

But even with these re-assurances, the idea of abandonment will haunt Steve forever.

In middle school, Steve's superior intelligence leads to general boredom and more mischief-making,

some dangerous. He is sent home from school many times.

Luckily, his 4th-grade math teacher notices

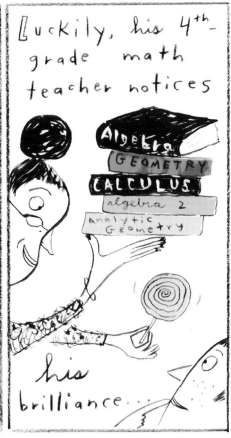

his brilliance...

IMOGENE HILL

...and keeps S T E V E challenged.

Outgoing and always curious, Steve makes friends with some of the neighborhood engineers.

14

chapter

2

Growing Up

(1965 – 1971)

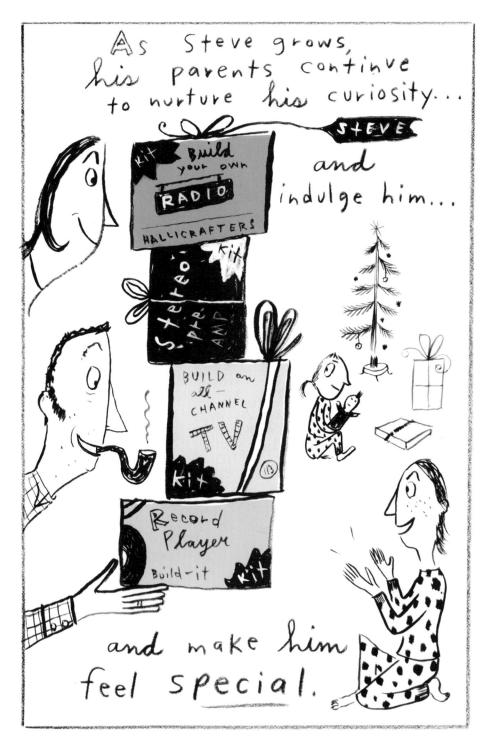

As Steve grows, his parents continue to nurture his curiosity... and indulge him... and make him feel special.

STEVE

Kit Build your own RADIO HALLICRAFTERS

Kit Stereo pre-amp

BUILD an all-CHANNEL TV Kit

Record Player Build-it Kit

Things are pretty low-tech:

These vinyl discs, called records, hold just a few songs, and you play them on an electric...

The records are carried around in a case like this.

17

...record player.

Big records, called LPs, for "long-playing"— 33.3 revolutions per minute— have a small hole.

transistor radios

made in Japan

Small records, called 45s, for the spin speed— 45 RPM— have a big hole.

Tech in thingamajig 19

Games are all *Candy Land* the board type.

These mini antennae are called rabbit ears.

Some TVs have a round screen.

Most TVs are just in B&W with no remote control.

I ♥ LOVE LUCY

(As with Wi-Fi now, the TV picture comes through the air.

18

All phones are the rotary-dial type with cords.

No cell phones!

Cameras require film and developing.

If you have to write something official, you use a typewriter.

To correct mistakes, you use a special kind of eraser or paint.

No ONE has a computer in their home.

No Internet!

No Google.

When Steve is 12, he decides to build a frequency counter,* which will help him with electronics projects.

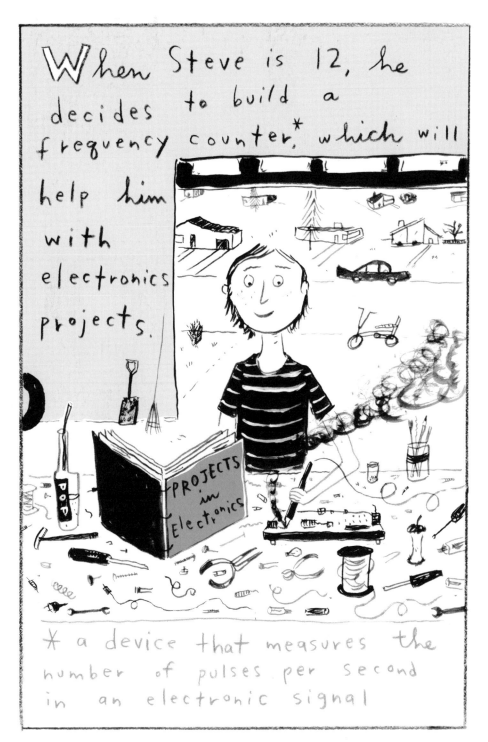

PROJECTS in Electronics

* a device that measures the number of pulses per second in an electronic signal

But he's missing some critical parts. Steve is not shy. He looks up his neighbor, the cofounder of Hewlett-Packard, in the phone book.

May I please speak to Mr. Bill Hewlett?

Hewlett gives Steve the parts he needs and, when summer comes, offers him a summer job.

Steve works on an assembly line making frequency counters.

Over the next 3 summers, he has a newspaper route and works at a large electronics store.

HEWLETT-PACKARD

H-P

Star Trek

HALTEK

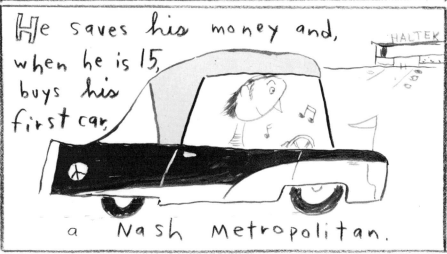

He saves his money and, when he is 15, buys his first car,

HALTEK

a Nash Metropolitan.

24

He reads piles of books, both old and new.

KING LEAR

MOBY-DICK

Dylan Thomas

Plato

He smokes pot and takes hallucinogenic drugs like LSD.

Blonde on Blonde

The high school electronics class is outta sight!

26

Through a friend in the class, Steve meets another Steve— Stephen Wozniak, aka Woz.

Heathkits!

Fibonacci numbers!

BOB Dylan!

Hallicrafters!

Electronics pranks!

Frequency counters!

Boolean algebra!

The San Jose swap meet!

They have a lot in common.

By now, Steve is a high school senior.

Woz is 4 years older, and already in college nearby at UC Berkeley. He's a real techno-whiz, and is shy and sweet-natured.

27

The same year, Steve meets the girl who will become his first serious girlfriend.

Chrisann Brennan

They make an animated film together...

...and with Woz get jobs entertaining children for $3 an hour

WESTGATE SHOPPING MALL

at a local shopping mall.

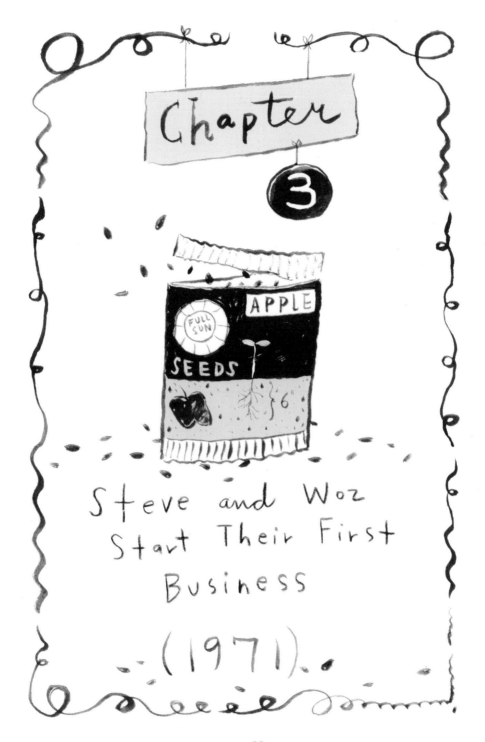

Chapter

③

Steve and Woz
Start Their First
Business

(1971).

One day Steve and Woz read a magazine article called "Secrets of the Little Blue Box." A blue box is a homemade, cobbled-together device that replicates sounds the phone company uses to connect long-distance calls. It is illegal.

In 1971, making long-distance calls is really expensive.

A hacker nicknamed Captain Crunch outsmarts the phone company by imitating the crucial tones with a whistle he finds in a box of cereal.

Other phone phreaks

use exotic birds.

We can try and make our own version of the blue box.

According to this article, everything we need to know is explained in a tech journal you can get at the library.

Let's go!

These devices would not work with today's phone system.

The phone company has already asked all libraries to remove this journal from their shelves...

...or cut out the page with the tone codes.

But Steve and Woz know an obscure library that might have the publication intact.

STANFORD LINEAR ACCELERATOR

LIBRARY

employee entrance

They sneak in on a Sunday when the library is closed.

Do you think it will still be there?

They do some reading...

and some shopping...

sunnyvale electronics

and by Thanksgiving their blue box prototype is ready to test.

RADIO shack

Will it work?

33

34

Steve makes sure the blue boxes are "user-friendly" so that anyone can use them, not just techy types. They happily sell them here and there until something really bad happens...

chapter

4

COLLEGE

and

Enlightenment

(1972 - 1974)

Steve's parents want him to go to college, although Steve is not sure about the idea.

Steve, honey?

SF State

U.C. Berkeley

De Anza Comm. College

For financial reasons, they hope he'll choose an affordable public university.

He wants someplace artsy and only applies to one school — an expensive private one.

REED

In September 1972, Steve goes off to Reed College in Portland, Oregon.

REED

After one semester he drops out.

It's too expensive. And I want to study what I want to study, not all this other stuff.

Groovy.

I hear you, man.

Dan Kottke

Still, he hangs around Reed sitting in on some courses. He especially likes a calligraphy class.

serif

sans serif

ascender →

baseline ↑

apple ←

x-height {

descender

Fonts

A @ A A

size: 28 pt
leading: 48 pt

nib →

INK

soda

return 5¢

To earn some money, he returns soda bottles and collects the deposits — 5¢ each.

39

1974

Steve leaves college and spends time on a commune on an apple orchard in Oregon.

He savors the art of pruning: cutting and trimming trees to make them grow stronger.

He becomes a vegetarian and eats so many carrots he turns orange! Because of this diet, he (wrongly!) believes he does not need to bathe much.

41

After 18 months in Oregon, Steve moves back home...

...and tries to get a job...

...at Atari, a computer game maker.

RECEPTION

I'm not leaving till you hire me.

Nolan Bushnell, president

Who is this kid?

42

He gets hired as a technician for $5 an hour,

but because he never bathes, he is made the lone employee on the night shift.

Steve works on game design. Like all computer games in 1974, Atari games are simple: no instruction manual is needed.

BE HERE NOW

Steve really likes that.

circa **1970** coin-operated
computer games **all in B&W only**

PONG

First commercially successful video game. Like table tennis on a screen.

SPACE RACE

Two players each control a rocket ship, avoiding obstacles.

TANK

Players guide their tanks around a maze, firing at obstacles.

These games are played only in arcades, as people do not have home computers yet.

46

49

Steve likes to take long walks while he's thinking.

INDIA

Calm the mind.

Simplicity.

Tune out distractions.

BOOKS cafe RESTAURANT SHOES HEAD SHOP

He still feels restless.

Natural FOOD SALE! HEAD Shoppe candle

I wonder if I should travel again, far and wide?

You know the Zen saying: "If you are willing to travel around the world to meet a teacher, one will appear next door."

chapter

5

Apple Is Born

(1975 - 1976)

Steve meditates in the mornings, audits physics classes at Stanford University in the afternoons, dreams of starting his own business, and goes back to work at Atari.

54

His boss offers much advice.

Pretend to be completely in control and people will assume you are.

Don't take **NO** for an answer.

Meanwhile, at Hewlett-Packard, Woz is frustrated designing calculators.

He has a new idea.

It's my prototype for something called a home computer.

Not interested.

It's not a serious computer.

It's just for hobbyists.

H-P may not like Woz's idea, but Steve does.

Insanely great, man! Let's start a business!

1801

Jacquard loom

← woven fabric

A [Very]

HIS

of the

before

punch cards

(punch cards later used in computers)

(one of the first programmable devices)

Origin of the word "bug": when an early computer stopped working, a moth was found inside.

Used in the 1890 US Census

HOLLERITH

electric tabulating system

ENIAC

1940s

Used in WWII to calculate bullet trajectories

Some of the first computers were used by the government to help with the census.

BRIEF

TORY

Computer

1975

1935

ENIGMA

German
encryption
machine

Breaking enemy
codes was a
big challenge for
the Allies
during WWII

1962

minuteman
guidance
computer

ICBM

inter-
continental
ballistic
missile

yet more
military uses

microprocessor 1971

Allows computers to
become cheaper
and smaller.

email 1971 the first
message
sent

And still, in
1975, only universities,
large companies, and
the government
have computers. Authorized
Personnel
Only
They are HUGE and
kept in separate areas
called DATA CENTERS.

DATA CENTER

19 75

DO NOT
ENTER

58

Almost no one has a computer at work or in their home.

In the early 1970s, powerful computers are HUGE, since memory takes up a lot of space. The ginormous computer shown here would hold only 8 megabytes* of memory.

In 2015, 64,000 megabytes fit in a cell phone.

*more about bytes on pages 70-71

59

They decide to raise money to buy parts to build a prototype.

Steve sells his VW bus for $1,500.

Woz sells his Hewlett-Packard calculator for $500.

Steve and Woz want their computer to be easy to use, nicely designed, AND inexpensive—

like the simple, modern home Steve grew up in.

Except for one man who owns a small chain of stores, the audience is not impressed.

Interesting. Keep in touch, boys!

You bet.

SLAC

HOMEBREW Co

The very next day Steve stops by...

BYTE shop

Hi— I'm keeping in touch!

... and makes a sale.

OK— I'll take 50 Apples, but I don't want build-it-yourself computer kits. I need them assembled.

PAUL TERRELL

Parts

Sure, OK. Whatever you'd like.

Homebrew CLUB meetings at SLAC

An assembly line is set up in the Jobs family home.

Steve does the soldering. Woz assembles boards.

Sister Patty helps, too. Mom answers the phone.

dylan

LOVE

2066

Another friend does the bookKeeping.

Dan packs the assembled computers into boxes...

...after they've been tested by Dad.

Steve delivers the finished product.

Here it is —

APPLE 1

computer

The **processor** is the brain of the computer.

Memory is where data and instructions are stored.

A **program** is a sequence of instructions a computer can interpret and execute.

Pixel is short for "picture element." Pixels are the dots that make up each image.

A P P L E

There is heavy use of the arrow keys to get where you want to be on the screen — no one has invented the mouse yet.

So tedious!

Graphics are crude in 1976, because unlike today, the pixels are HUGE.

H O U S E

D O G

Images are mostly in black-and-white. Very few colors, if any.

One **byte** is one character — like a 1 or a Z or a %.

An operating system (OS) is the master program that runs the whole computer.

Booting up

means loading software from the disc/tape into RAM memory.

* RAM * (random-access memory) is where programs actually "run."

* ROM * (read-only memory) are the programming routines that are "burned" into permanent memory.

a Koa wood case made by a local cabinet maker

one kilobyte (KB) is 1,024 characters— roughly one page of text.

one megabyte (MB) is 1,048,576 characters— roughly a whole book.

one gigabyte (GB) is 1,073,741,824 characters. Roughly 1,000 books— a whole shelf.

one terabyte (TB) is 1,099,511,627,776 characters. Roughly 1,000,000 books— a whole library.

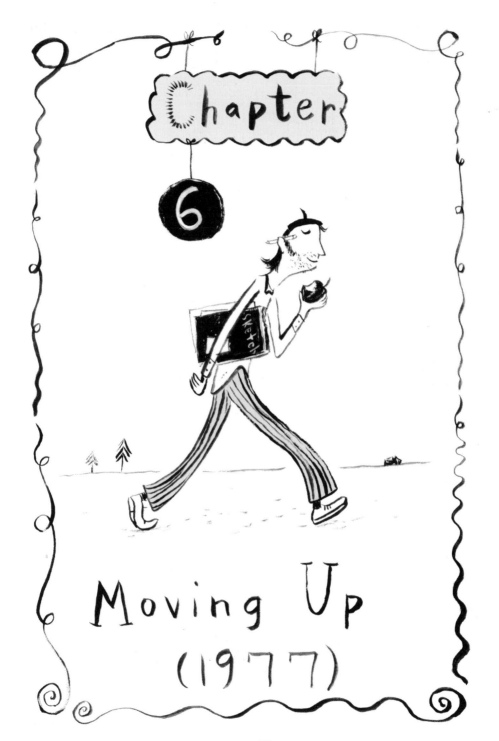

Chapter

6

Moving Up
(1977)

The Apples are selling, but only to a limited market of hobbyists and other techy types. **1**

Steve and Woz understand that for their company to grow, they need to make some changes. So... **2**

...they hire more people. Engineers, programmers. There are now 12 employees. **3**

They rent office space nearby, in Cupertino. **4**

Because they need more money, they find an investor.

MIKE MARKKULA

Apple is now valued at #5,309. **5**

Markkula will give them cash in exchange for part ownership of Apple. **6**

Steve is 21 years old; Woz is 26. Markkula, 34, has already retired from the tech industry — a millionaire. He is good at marketing and sales and will help them get their business going.

Steve really likes his attitude.

You know, you should never start a company with the goal of getting rich. Your goal should be making something you believe in and building a company that will last.

For the next Apple, Steve wants to break out of the hobbyist market and design a computer that will appeal to a wider audience. It should fit in an attractive case and have a built-in keyboard. This has never been done before.

Steve goes to the mall to study the design of small kitchen appliances.

(fake wood grain is popular)

Brady Bunch

what's

LATE 19

tech

color TVs with remote control

♫ clock radios

1200

home video games to use with your TV

music is on compact cassettes

sony walkman

Polaroid SX-70 cameras

78

Meanwhile, using all his wizardry, Woz is designing the INSIDE of the computer, figuring out how to make it work better— and faster.

He has finally quit his job at Hewlett-Packard.

Boys, you need a marketing plan, a logo, etc.

You can't keep peddling these things door-to-door, you know.

Steve and Woz hire a publicity firm to help them promote their company.

blue

Regis McKenna

A designer named Rob Janoff designs a logo.

It has rainbow stripes.

green

Pink

Steve likes this quote, thought to come from artist Leonardo da Vinci:

"Simplicity is the ultimate sophistication."

yellow

Steve's new personal look is same.

clothes from Wilkes Bashford, a fancy store in San Francisco

1966 R 60/2 BMW motorcycle

84

Woz has become a lot less involved in Apple.

BERKELEY

After recovering from a flying accident, he decides to go back to college.

Steve and Woz have launched the entire personal computer industry, thanks to ingenuity, hard work, and being in the right place at the right time. By the end of 1978, Apple's sales are over $7.9 million.

La Honda Road

Over the next 16 years, close to 6 million Apple IIs will be sold!

Chapter

7

Moving
On

(1978 - 1981)

In May 1978, Steve has a baby girl with his old girlfriend Chrisann. But he's irritated with the responsibility and

The baby's name is Lisa.

does not want to be involved.

He wants only to focus on his new business

and think about the next computer.

1979

The Apple II is not going to be a hit forever.

How to improve it?

All across the US, and especially in Silicon Valley, many companies — big and small — employ scientists, engineers, and designers in research labs.

IBM

XEROX PARC

DEC

BELL LABS N.J.

NASA AMES

They are all busy developing ideas for the office of the future. Xerox PARC* is in the forefront — even though they're not known for making computers.

*Palo Alto Research Center

Steve hears about some of these ideas.

Xerox PARC wow! Amazing NEW — Scientific American

We've gotta get over to PARC.

Bill Atkinson, Apple engineer

At about the same time, Xerox's venture capital division in Connecticut gives Apple a call. Like many, they want to invest in the hot new computer company.

Steve licks his chops.

OK-So here's the deal: I'll let you invest a million dollars in Apple if you show us what's going on at Xerox PARC. You gotta share everything with us.

No problem.

The Connecticut office has no idea how valuable Xerox PARC's research is.

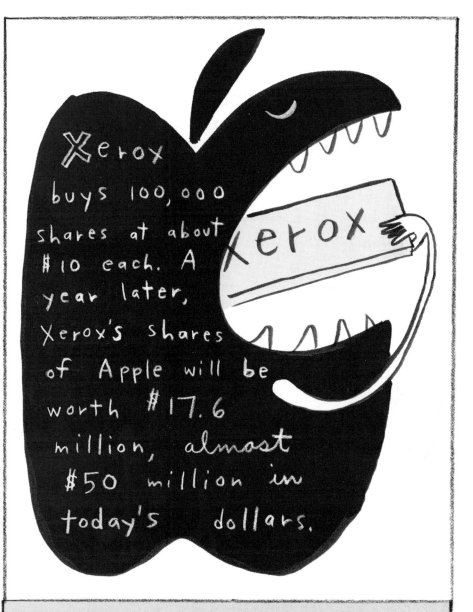

Xerox buys 100,000 shares at about $10 each. A year later, Xerox's shares of Apple will be worth $17.6 million, almost $50 million in today's dollars.

Still, Apple gets the better part of the deal.

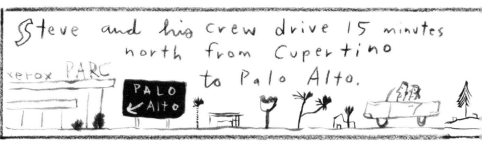

Steve and his crew drive 15 minutes north from Cupertino to Palo Alto.

We call it GUI. Say "gooey."

Advances in Computing

graphical
User
interface

networking

object-oriented programming

drop-down menus

As promised, the scientists show him what they've been working on.

These are all brand-new ideas to make the computers of the future simpler and easier to use. They are groundbreaking!

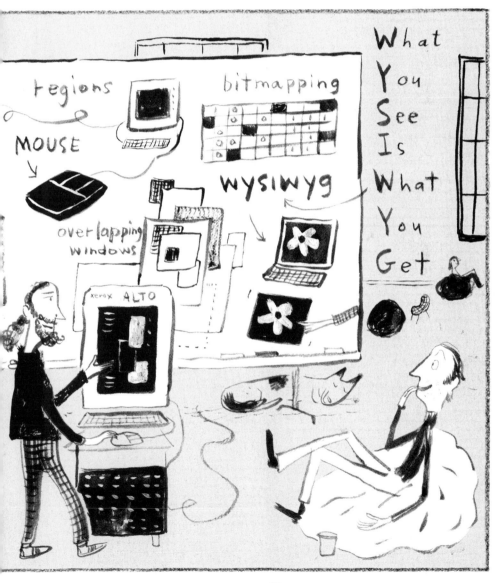

regions

bitmapping

MOUSE

wysiwyg

overlapping windows

xerox ALTO

What
You
See
Is
What
You
Get

1980 By September, 130,000 Apple IIs have been sold.

There are now more than 1,000 employees, and the company occupies 15 buildings.

With the new technology and ideas from Xerox PARC, and a new computer in the works, it's time to GO PUBLIC.

Apple is a highly successful young company with thousands of loyal users, and people clamor to buy shares of stock.

Apple's value goes up quickly. By the end of December, it is valued at $1.79 BILLION.

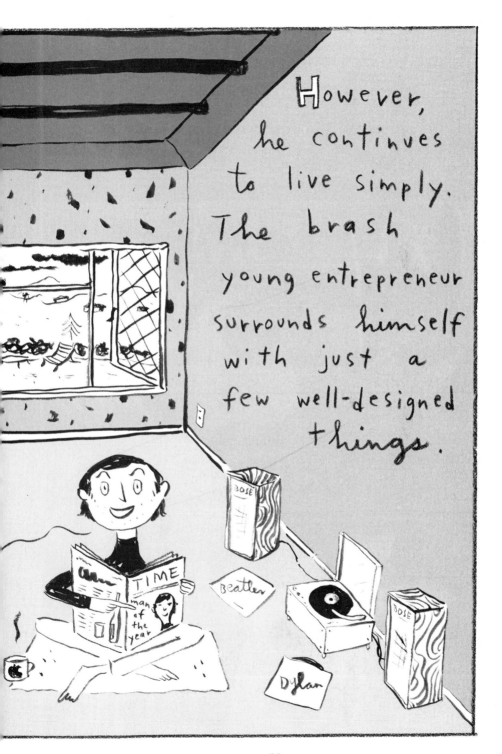

However, he continues to live simply. The brash young entrepreneur surrounds himself with just a few well-designed things.

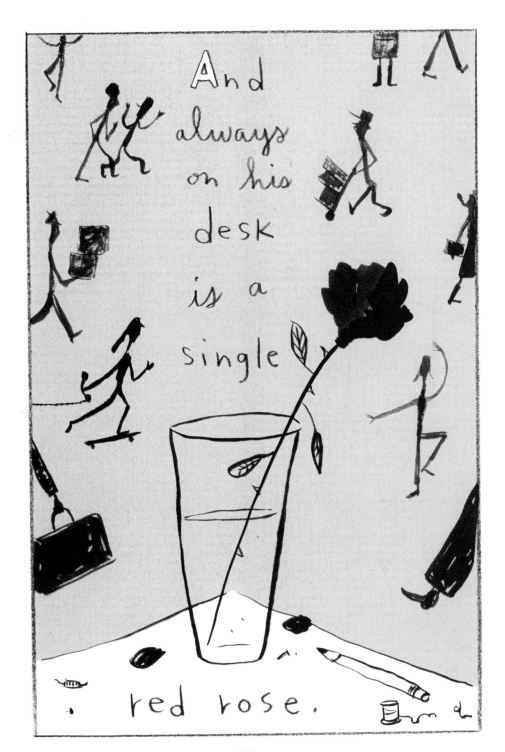

And
always
on his
desk
is a
single

red rose.

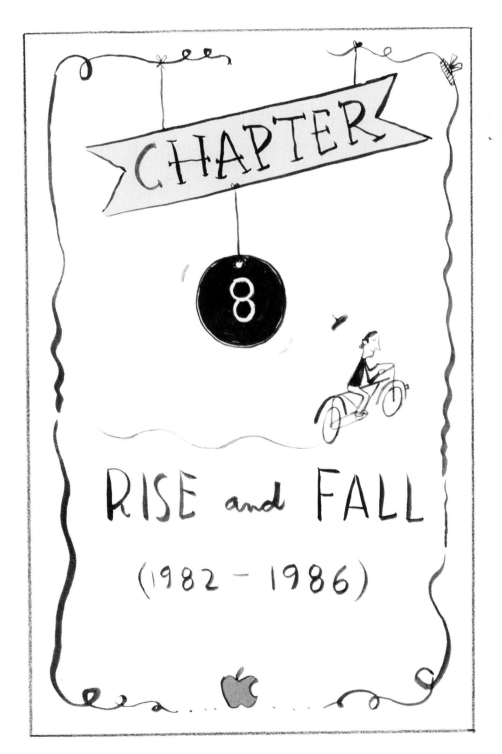

CHAPTER

8

RISE and FALL

(1982 – 1986)

Long a follower of Zen Buddhism and a great admirer of the Japanese design aesthetic, Steve travels to Japan...

and appreciates the serenity and sublime order of the temples and gardens of Kyoto...

and the busyness and zaniness of Tokyo.

KABUKI! N H 東京 (東京) NHK UC SONY
NIKON SEIBU TOKYU HANDS
SHINJUKU GINZA: SHIBUYA
SUSHI PACHINKO ueno YAKITORI

He goes to a pristine Sony factory and sees the workers all in uniform...

... and finally to see designer Issey Miyake,

Konichiwa!

who designs for Steve a...

uNiform!

black
turtlenecks,
hundreds of
them,
all the
same

New Balance
sneakers

blue jeans

Steve Jobs
the paper doll

Steve is still concerned with the OUTSIDE of the computer. He's becoming even more involved with the design.

Simplify.

It must be intuitively obvious.

The radius of the first chamfer* needs to be bigger.

Less is more.

It's too boxy.

I don't like the size of the bevel.*

More curvaceous.

* see page 118

Work continues, but these are harder times for Apple. Other companies, like IBM, have entered the personal computer industry.

should we buy our PCs from the giant IBM or that small new company named after a piece of fruit?

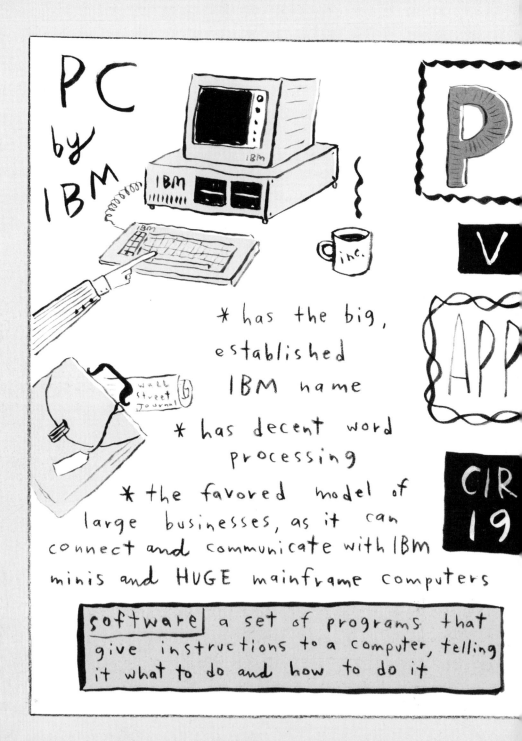

PC
by IBM

* has the big, established IBM name

* has decent word processing

* the favored model of large businesses, as it can connect and communicate with IBM minis and HUGE mainframe computers

software a set of programs that give instructions to a computer, telling it what to do and how to do it

P V APP CIR 19

APPLE II

* has VisiCalc, a terrific program for visualizing spreadsheets

* offers pioneering programs for writing and making music

* has games, graphics, and educational software

* the favored model of schools and universities

hardware| the physical pieces of a computer

OK, so we need new leadership here at Apple. How about someone with lots of experience running a BIG company?

Steve likes to take long walks while having important discussions. He goes to New York City and tries to interest John Sculley, the CEO of Pepsi, to come to Apple to be its president.

While Steve knows himself to be quirky, tactless, confrontational, and insensitive, he knows Sculley is polite, polished, and easygoing. These qualities could help Apple grow and deal with competition from other computer companies.

I'm pretty happy working for Pepsi! And I don't know anything about computers.

Sculley finds Steve brilliant and fascinating. He's flattered that Steve wants him at Apple and decides to change jobs.

Sculley comes on board, but right away there are disagreements.

Being the boss of an established soda company is mostly about putting out the same product year after year. Running a high-tech company is about improving, innovating, and trying to come up with the next big thing.

This is called a storyboard.

Steve wants his ad to show the world how Apple products are tools for creativity, COOL and slightly rebellious!

The inspiration for the new Apple commercial is George Orwell's novel about a...

...totalitarian future society of government surveillance, constant war, and

mind control headed by the tyrannical leader Big Brother.

Steve gets his way...

... and when the ad is aired, it's called.

A sensation!

The greatest commercial ever made!

On January 24, Apple Computer will introduce Macintosh. And you'll see why 1984 won't be like 1984.

Macs sell well right from the start, but Apple is facing increased competition from other companies. Most aggressive is Microsoft, a software-only business led by the young Bill Gates.

microsoft

apple

NeRdY

StYliSH

born in 1955

born in 1955

company produces only software

college dropout (Harvard)

college dropout (Reed)

company makes hardware AND software

BiLL GATES

STEVE JOBS

122

We recommend that steve quit running the macintosh group and start a research group at Apple.

Good idea.

This is a better use of steve.

Apple's board of directors

Confine his craziness to one small part of the company.

Apple has approximately 6,500 employees now, roughly 700 in the mac division.

Steve considers this new role.

Hmmmm... run a lab for new products and ideas. Could be good.

But he decides he can't live with a smaller role in the company HE founded.

123

He becomes so nasty and unreasonable, so difficult to work with, that in the end, the board members and other employees choose Sculley as boss.

Steve quietly sells all but one share of his Apple stock, worth about $100 million, or $217 million today. In 1986, shares trade for $4 each.

At 30 years old, he is a very rich man — but rather miserable, too.

He travels to Europe, thinking about what to do NEXT...

How about starting a new company called NeXT?

The new computer will be a CUBE.

The logo is a CUBE, too...

I'm Paul Rand!

...designed by a famous designer. Steve pays $100,000.

It will be much faster than a PC and be able to do more things.

The company has 8 employees.

The target market is university research labs.

't's

Ring! Ring! Ring!

Motorola DynaTAC 8000x

Cordless phones

mobile phones — few people have them since they cost thousands of dollars!

80s

Microwave ovens

Smart modems using phone lines to communicate with computers

Beta tapes

MAC

NeXT computer

desktop publishing

$6,500

NeXT struggles. Steve's perfectionism delays and delays the on-sale date of the computer.

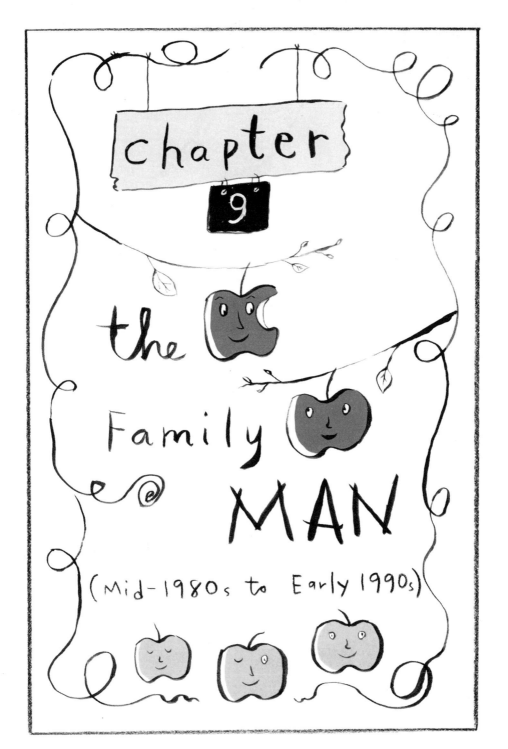

chapter

9

the

Family

MAN

(Mid-1980s to Early 1990s)

1989 As the CEO of NeXT Computer,

STANFORD Business SCHOOL

Steve is asked to give a talk.

While he is waiting to go onstage, he meets a young Stanford business student.

She jokes,

I won a raffle and **YOU** get to take me out to dinner after your talk.

Oh, yeah?

But afterward, Steve has a business meeting to rush to.

bye

bye

As he is about to leave, he thinks,

If this were my last night on earth, would I want to spend it at a meeting or with this woman?

Ooo

134

135

Wait! Laura? Laurene? Let's have dinner NOW.

She's a down-to-earth vegetarian, and very grounded, too; a good balance for Steve's eccentricities.

They marry in 1991, and later that year their son, Reed, is born.

Steve's daughter, Lisa, now 13, has become a part of the family, too.

They all live fairly simply in an old house in Palo Alto.

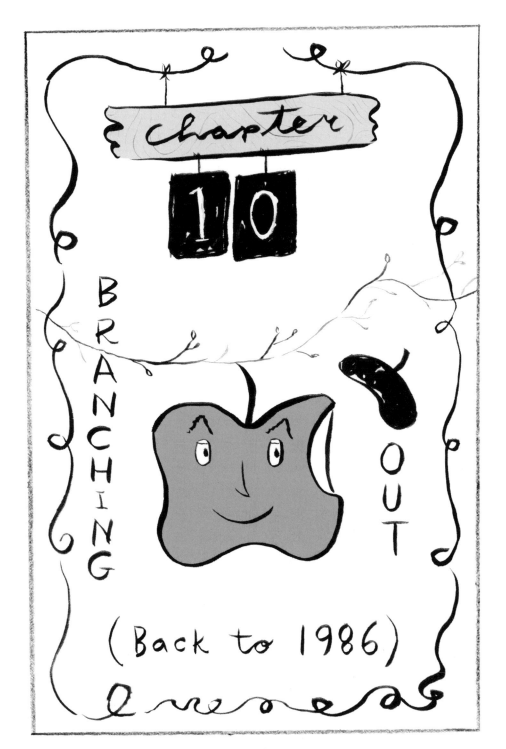

chapter

10

BRANCHING

OUT

(Back to 1986)

While still running NeXT, which is tanking, Steve buys Pixar for $5 million ($10.7 million today) and immediately invests another $5 million to keep it going.

Art and technology together—just what I love!

Zillions more colors and pixels than most computers.

Render Man
Animation on a computer!
$30,000

It's a small, pioneering computer graphics company that makes fancy computers and the software to go with them.

I think there's a market! Everyone will want one!

Images can be rendered in 3-D.

But the computers are VERY expensive and don't sell.

Steve keeps pouring his own money into the company to keep it afloat.

138

139

The short film, called *Luxo Jr.*, about a lamp, wins some awards.

SIGGRAPH* BEST Film 1986

*an annual computer graphics conference

Pixar gets new business creating animation for TV commercials. But not enough. The company is going broke.

The animation department has an idea for another short film.

It's about tin toys!

You need $300,000 to produce it?

Steve is skeptical.

The little 5-minute film — about toys that come to life — wins the Oscar for Best Animated Short Film, the first computer-animated film to do so.

OSCAR ANIMATED SHORT FILM 1988

Disney is very excited about this new kind of animation and tries to woo former employee Lasseter back.

Sorry, I'm loyal to Pixar now.

Then Steve has an even BIGGER idea.

What if we make a feature film, COMPUTER-animated, in the Disney tradition?

No one has done this before.

As Walt Disney liked to say, "It's Kind of fun to do the impossible."

But Pixar is now almost bankrupt and needs funding to make an expensive feature film.

We need MONEY.

OK, we're going to collaborate.

Disney gets rights to characters, film sequels, etc, etc.

Jeffrey Katzenberg

Steve has to accept their deal because Pixar needs Disney a lot more than Disney needs Pixar.

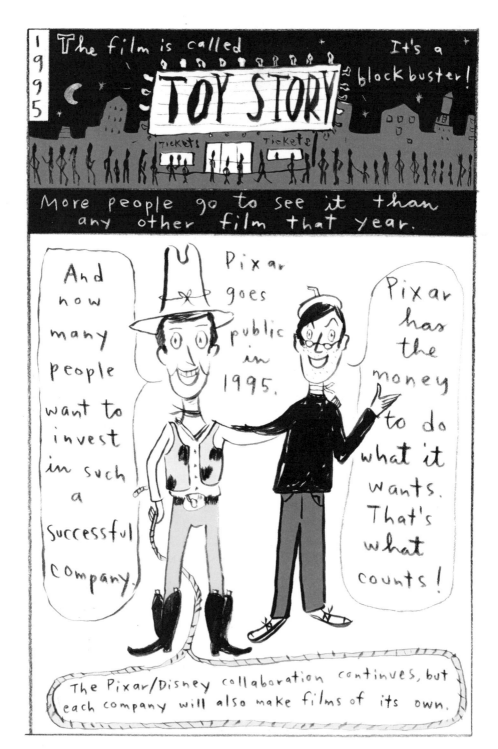

1995

The film is called TOY STORY It's a blockbuster!

Tickets   Tickets

More people go to see it than any other film that year.

And now many people want to invest in such a successful company.

Pixar goes public in 1995.

Pixar has the money to do what it wants. That's what counts!

The Pixar/Disney collaboration continues, but each company will also make films of its own.

Steve's Pixar stock is now worth an astonishing #1.2 BILLION.

But Steve continues to live simply.

There's no yacht in my future.* I've never done this for the money!

* Ha! see pages 206 - 207

When Pixar expands, Steve designs their new building with a huge central atrium for workers to meet and mingle.

atrium

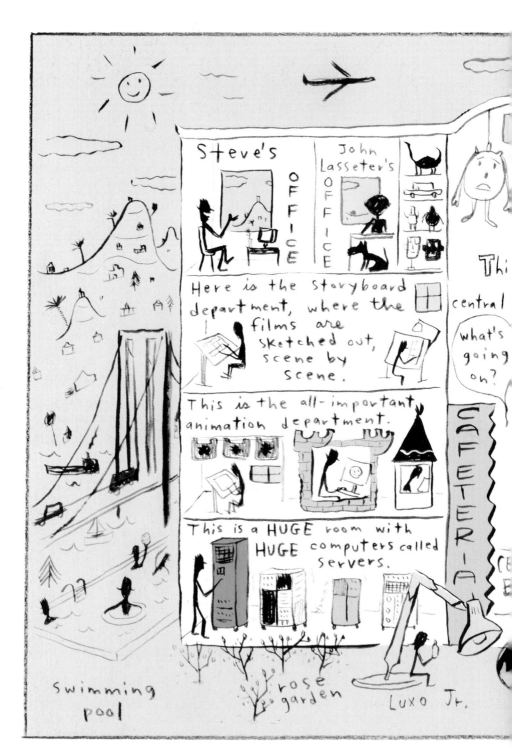

Steve's OFFICE

John Lasseter's OFFICE

Here is the storyboard department, where the films are sketched out, scene by scene.

This is the all-important animation department.

This is a HUGE room with HUGE computers called servers.

central

what's going on?

CAFETERIA

swimming pool

rose garden

Luxo Jr.

149

2006 The contract between Pixar and Disney is coming to an end.

While Disney/Pixar have released megahits, Disney on its own has made multiple animation megaflops.

PIXAR FINDING NEMO
CK.T.S TICKETS
DISNEY BROTHER DISNEY BEAR
Tickets

Robert Iger

The new Disney CEO approaches Steve and wants to buy Pixar.

Steve puts together a clever deal and Disney buys Pixar for $7.4 billion.

Pixar gets stronger.

Disney gets better.

WOW, Dad!

Awesome!

Insanely great!

PIXAR
RATATOUILLE
DISNEY
2007

Disney/Pixar goes on to win more than 25 Academy Awards. It has become the most successful animation studio in the world.

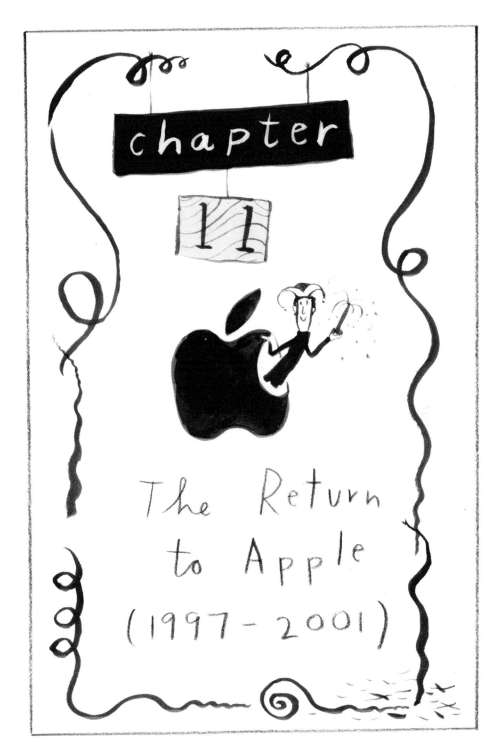

chapter

11

The Return
to Apple
(1997 - 2001)

1997 Steve is still running a booming Pixar and a tanking NeXT.

Meanwhile, back at Apple...

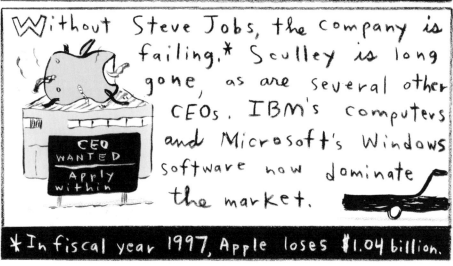

Without Steve Jobs, the company is failing.* Sculley is long gone, as are several other CEOs. IBM's computers and Microsoft's Windows software now dominate the market.

CEO WANTED Apply within

*In fiscal year 1997, Apple loses $1.04 billion.

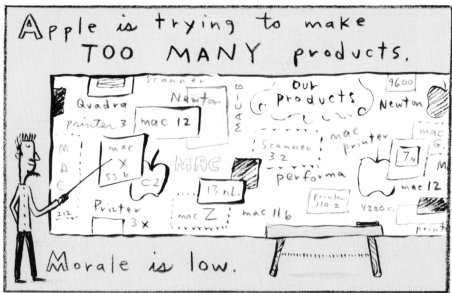

Apple is trying to make TOO MANY products.

Our products

Morale is low.

And because Apple likes the innovative way

Insanely great!

the NeXT computers work, it buys NeXT.

Everyone assumes Steve will play a minor role,

but...

... he has bigger plans than that!

And after being gone for 12 years, he makes a triumphant return.

Of course, everyone at Apple remembers how difficult Steve can be, but they also remember his vision and his creativity.

Badly managed Apple is now close to bankruptcy, and the board of directors and employees are pretty desperate. Initially a part-time advisor, Steve is soon given more and more power.

He fires many, many people and cuts way, way back on the number of products Apple makes.

More drawings are made on paper...

...designs are made on computer,

and 3-D models are formed by an amazing machine!

3-D model-O-MATIC

And finally, extensive research is done

Jelly Bean Factory

Jelly Belly

on color translucency.

Here it is →

DESIGN STUDIO

The people who are crazy enough to think they can change the world are the ones who do.

THINK Different

Think Different

groundbreaking ad campaign featuring celebrities and other influential people

a candy-colored, translucent, mouth-watering, jelly bean-influenced, cheeky, scrumptious, good-enough-to-eat, brand-new iMac!

The price is $1,299.

New iMac

What's late

boxy monitor

email really hits mainstream

DVDs

Klutzy CD tray

Google is founded.

WWW is growing rapidly.

digital cameras

NEW!
1990s

SONY

SONY
PlayStation

netflix
FILM
DVDs by Mail

eBay
online
auction

Mobile
phones are
smaller and
more affordable
but complicated
to use.

a complicated
mess of portable music players

SONY
MD

300

mini
discs

MP3 is a compressed
digital format.

As work continues, Steve has an idea to open stores that sell only Apple products.

He wants to control the Apple customer's shopping experience.

Steve, maybe we should have a focus group?

Test out the market and see if people might actually shop in an Apple store or buy one of these?

Did Alexander Graham Bell do any market research before he invented the TELEPHONE?

APPLE STORE

And Henry Ford liked to say, "If I'd asked them what they wanted, they would have told me, 'A faster horse!'"

Steve secretly builds a store prototype *inside* a warehouse and makes regular visits to fine-tune the look and feel.

He designs an innovative translucent staircase and gets the patent for it.

He imports special sandstone from Italy for the floors.

Buon giorno!

Italia

Ron Johnson

Steve, I have an idea. We can have experts on hand at a special counter and call them geniuses.

I don't like your idea. And they're geeks!

167

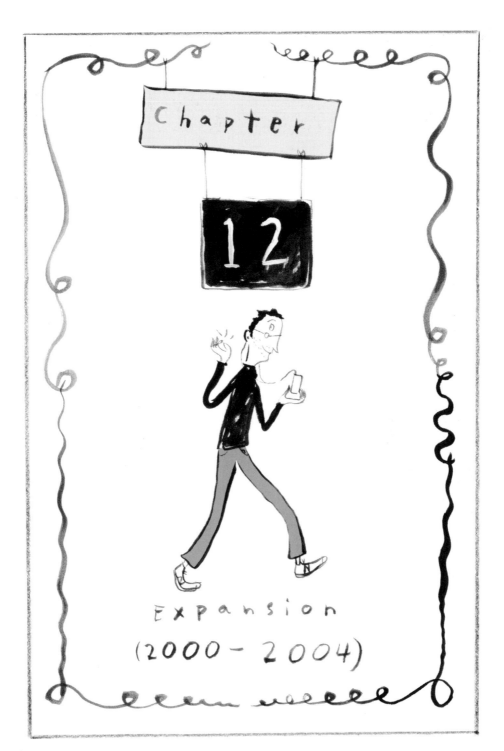

Chapter

12

Expansion

(2000 - 2004)

Steve, always trying to improve the
Apple product consumer experience,
develops a cable for digital data
called firewire, and some cool new
activities — called applications — like

i Photo
i Movie

Final Cut Pro,
i DVD,
Garage Band
and...

iMAC

(What does the i-something stand for?
Individual, instant, inform, inspire, and Internet)

... iTunes!

Always a HUGE music fan (he loves the Beatles and Bob Dylan), Steve comes out with a clever new way to manage, mix, and enjoy music.

You can listen to your music on your computer and you can upload it, sort it, make playlists, and listen to the radio, too!

WOW—and visuals that go with the music! Cool! This comes included on the Mac when you buy it?

YUP

Too bad the portable music devices are all badly designed and user-unfriendly.

Back home and pining for Japanese food, Steve sends the Apple cafeteria chef to the Tsukiji Soba Academy in Japan for training.

TSUKIJI

With the new technology bought from Toshiba,

the tiny drives

Apple's designers and engineers work together on a SECRET new product.

What can it be?

Yes, Steve can be ultra-convincing. If you've been told (unrealistically) that you can get the prototype out overnight or present 10 new ideas for the meeting tomorrow...

...you've entered Steve's famous "reality distortion field."

An engineer presents the prototype that he's been working on for weeks—

day and night, night and day.

It's too heavy!

Too clunky!

See the bubbles coming up? There's AIR in there!

First Steve sells one record company on the idea. Then another comes on board.

Some ask for a % of iPod sales. No way!

some recording artists object:

No unbundling of MY albums!

My contract forbids that sort of thing.

NO deconstructing!

But it is too late. Everyone knows that piracy has been going on for months and Steve's innovations are necessary.

Steve travels around and shows off how easy it is to use the iTunes store.

And then some musicians decide they really like the idea.

Looky, looky.... Man, somebody FINALLY got it right!

Recording artists and music producers finally sign on. Steve gets the record companies to sell their songs online in the iTunes store, and gets music lovers to pay for what they had been getting for free.

* Apple gets 29¢

This revolutionizes the music industry.

190

Chapter

13

COMPUTER

Refined
DESIGN
(2004-2011)

2007 — the family

Steve and Laurene now have 3 kids.

REED 15
ERIN 11
EVE 8

Steve's impeccable design sense is not left at the office. At home, when it comes time to buy a new washer, meetings are held and pros and cons debated.

193

Portable phones have been around for years.

194

But when Steve sees his first demo of multi-touch on a phone, he decides to forge ahead and not hold the technology back.

*using more than one finger at a time to do fancy stuff, like enlarge an image

This is the future !!

This is it !!

Jony Ive

Mobile phones spread worldwide.

What'

20

Wi-Fi — connecting to Internet without cable

Google becomes a verb.

USBs

ebooks

Kindle Nook

tablet — a handheld computer operated by a stylus or finger

New?

YouTube
Wikipedia
flash technology

iMac
Sunflower

'00s

Global
Positioning
System

Amazon –
online retailing
blogs

Texting
catches on.

Facebook
MySpace

iCloud,
a new way to
manage and sync
up data and
devices

Steve tries to keep his cancer battle a secret. He feels it's a personal matter,

AND he's worried about the public losing confidence in Apple.

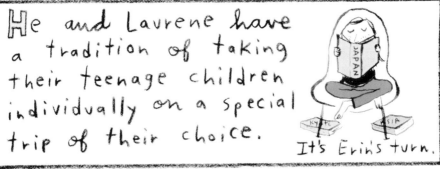

He and Laurene have a tradition of taking their teenage children individually on a special trip of their choice.

It's Erin's turn.

Steve is barely able to make it.

They travel to Japan and to a temple of 100 mosses.

Back home, Laurene tends a bountiful garden.

Steve works.

Steve's illness kills his appetite.

213

Your time is limited, so don't waste it living someone else's life.

Don't be trapped by dogma, which is living with the results of other people's thinking.

Don't let the noise of others' opinions drown out your own inner voice.

Acknowledgments

Thanks to Anne, Lee, Rachael, and Stephanie at Schwartz & Wade Books; my agent, Brenda Bowen; David Biedny for a top-notch tech overview and history; Nick Sung for a terrific tour; my assistants, Ellspeth Tremblay and Dingding Hu; Isabelle Dervaux; Anne Silverstein; siblings Andrea and Sammy Recalde; the Bellport, New York, library; and my two favorite people in the world, Carl and Sam Friedberg.

Bibliography

The teetering stack of material I've accumulated to write and illustrate this book is over four feet tall! In the pile are books, DVDs, photographs, maps, clippings, sketches, printouts, and magazines, including old copies of *Popular Electronics*, *Popular Mechanics*, and *Mechanix Illustrated* from the 1960s and 1970s. More specifically:

Brown, David W. "In Praise of Bad Steve." *The Atlantic*, October 6, 2011, theatlantic.com/technology /archive/2011/10/in-praise-of-bad-steve/246242/.

Elliot, Jay. *The Steve Jobs Way: iLeadership for a New Generation*. Philadelphia: Vanguard Press, 2011.

Goldsmith, Mike, and Tom Jackson. *Eyewitness COMPUTER*. New York: DK Publishing, 2011.

Goodell, Jeff. "Steve Jobs in 1994: The Rolling Stone Interview." *Rolling Stone*, June 16, 1994, rollingstone.com/culture/news/steve-jobs-in-1994-the-rolling-stone-interview-20110117.

Isaacson, Walter. *Steve Jobs*. New York: Simon and Schuster, 2011.

Jobs, Steve. Macworld Expo keynote address, 2007, youtube.com/watch?v=-QZKy9FzR6k.

———. Stanford University commencement address, June 12, 2005, youtube.com /watch?v=VHWUCX6osgM.

Manjoo, Farhad. "Jobs the Jerk." *Slate*, October 25, 2011, slate.com/articles/technology /technology/2011/10/steve_jobs_biography_the_new_book_doesn_t_explain_what_made _the_.html.

Markoff, John. "Apple Computer Co-Founder Strikes Gold with New Stock." *New York Times*, 30 November 1995, nytimes.com/1995/11/30/us/apple-computer-co-founder-strikes-gold -with-new-stock.html.

———. *What the Dormouse Said: How the Sixties Counterculture Shaped the Personal Computer Industry*. New York: Viking, 2005.

Moritz, Michael. *Return to the Little Kingdom: How Apple and Steve Jobs Changed the World*. New York: Overlook Press, 2009. Kindle edition.

Morris, Betsy. "Steve Jobs Speaks Out." *Fortune*, March 2008, money.cnn.com/galleries/2008 /fortune/0803/gallery.jobsqna.fortune/.

Morrow, Daniel. Smithsonian Institution Oral History interview with Steve Jobs, April 20, 1995, americanhistory.si.edu/comphist/sj1.html.

———. "Steve Jobs interview: One-on-one in 1995." *Computerworld*, April 1995, computerworld .com/s/article/9220609/Steve_Jobs_interview_One_on_one_in_1995.

Richards, Mark, and John Alderman. *Core Memory: A Visual Survey of Vintage Computers*. San Francisco: Chronicle Books, 2007.

Rosenbaum, Ron. "Secrets of the Little Blue Box," *Esquire*, October 1971, historyofphonephreaking .org/docs/rosenbaum1971.pdf.

Sheff, David. "Steven Jobs." *Playboy*, February 1985, longform.org/stories/playboy-interview-steve
-jobs.

Triumph of the Nerds: The Rise of Accidental Empires. Ambrose Video, 2002.

Wolf, Gary. "Steve Jobs: The Next Insanely Great Thing." *Wired*, February 1996, archive.wired.com
/wired/archive//4.02/jobs.html?person=steve_jobs&topic_set=wiredpeople.

To further research this book, and especially for the pictures, I visited Silicon Valley and drove on the 101 Freeway and along El Camino Real. I visited the Computer History Museum in Mountain View, and went to Palo Alto and the Stanford Linear Accelerator Laboratory. I saw where Xerox PARC once was, and I got a glimpse of the suburban garage in Los Altos where Apple Computer was born, as well as the Jobs family house in Palo Alto. Back up north in the San Francisco Bay Area, I was given a tour of Pixar. (Thanks, NS!)

Notes

Any quotes not mentioned below in the source notes are made up, with an intent to communicate a sense of what I imagine was said.

"Here's to the crazy ones": advertising copy partly written by Steve Jobs.

Chapter 1

On growing up in the early days of Silicon Valley: Isaacson, 1–20, and Smithsonian interview.

On middle-school teacher Imogen Hill: *Playboy* and *Computerworld*.

On Larry Lang: *Computerworld* and Smithsonian interview.

Chapter 2

On building a frequency counter: *Playboy* and Isaacson, 17.

Chapter 3

On the blue box: *Esquire*.

On building the blue box: Moritz, Chapter 6: "The Little Blue Box," and *Triumph of the Nerds*, Part 1.

On selling the blue boxes: *Playboy* and Isaacson, 29–30.

Chapter 4

On being at Reed College: Isaacson, 33–41.

"If today were the last day": Stanford University commencement address.

"I'm going to find my": Isaacson, 45.

"Live each day as if": *Fortune*.

On meeting with Zen master Kobun: Isaacson, 48–50.

Chapter 5

"Don't take no" and "Pretend to be": Isaacson, 55.

On computer history: the Computer History Museum, Goldsmith, and Richards.

On choosing a company name: Isaacson, 63, and Moritz, Chapter 10: "Half Right."

"I don't think it would have happened without": *Playboy*.

Chapter 6

On Markkula: Isaacson, 75–78, and Moritz, Chapter 12, "Mercedes and a Corvette."

On the early days of Apple and first uses of Apple IIs: Moritz, Chapter 18, "Welcome IBM, Seriously."

"You should never start a company": Isaacson, 78.

Chapter 7

On Xerox PARC: *Triumph of the Nerds*, Part 3.

Chapter 8

"If it could save a person's": *Triumph of the Nerds*, Part 3.

"Do you want to spend the rest of": *Triumph of the Nerds*, Part 3.

"Good artists imitate": *Triumph of the Nerds*, Part 3. (Steve Jobs attributed this quote to Pablo Picasso.)

On being ousted from Apple: Isaacson, 194–210.

On NeXT: "It's not late": Isaacson, 236.

Chapter 9
On finding his biological family and on meeting Laurene Powell: Isaacson, 250–283.

Chapter 10
On the early days of Pixar: Isaacson, 238–249.
"There's no yacht": *New York Times*.

Chapter 11
"Which one do I tell": Isaacson, 337.
"What kind of computer would the Jetsons": Isaacson, 352.
"Did Alexander Graham Bell": Isaacson, 170.
"Henry Ford liked to say": Elliott, 147.
On the design of the first Apple Store: Isaacson, 368–377.

Chapter 12
"There's no satisfying clicking": *Slate*.
On the development of the iPod: Isaacson, 490–510.
On tossing an iPod prototype into a fish tank: *The Atlantic*.
"What's on your iPod?": Isaacson, 497.

Chapter 13
On the history of cell phones and development of the iPhone: Elliott, 203–204.
"The phone will have only one": Elliott, 23, and *Fortune*.
On the design of the iPhone: Isaacson, 465–475.
"This is the future!": Isaacson, 468.
"Every once in a while a revolutionary product comes along": Macworld Expo
    keynote address.
On appliance shopping: *Wired*.
On designing the family yacht: Isaacson, 529.
"Your time is limited": Stanford University commencement address.

About the Author

Jessie Hartland is the author and illustrator of the highly acclaimed graphic biography *Bon Appétit: The Delicious Life of Julia Child,* which the *New York Times* described as "bursting with exuberant urban-naïf gouache paintings and a hand-lettered text that somehow manages to recount every second of Child's life." Her illustrations have appeared in newspapers and magazines throughout the world, including the *New York Times, Bon Appétit, Martha Stewart Living, Real Simple,* and *Travel + Leisure.* She is also a commercial artist whose work can be seen on ceramics and fabric, as well as in advertisements and store windows. She lives in New York City with her family. Visit her at jessiehartland.com.

SEP 2015